Copyright © 2017

A R. Neal

For more information about
the writing of the author, visit
www.preciousrelationships.com

Dedication

It is a blessing having great friends who truly love God, which is a reflection of their lifestyles. It is often said, "People are in your life for a reason, season, or lifetime." Therefore, I do not take true friendships for granted.

Because of her continued support and love throughout the writing of this book, I thank D. Elaine McNease, my sister, for being totally dedicated in assisting me.

To Jalessa Sheppard who has assisted me in various ways. Most of all she inspires me by believing in my vision. "J" is a very talented young lady and I look forward to continue working with her.

To Mr. James Ruth, a faithful follower and supporter. I thank you for encouraging and believing in me.

To Mr. Samuel Banks, a genuine friend, and confidant who is supportive. I appreciate your knowledge and encouragement.

God has placed some great women in my life, two of which have transitioned. These women exemplify the true meaning of being virtuous women.

For Deborah Sadie Cook and Mikal Turk,

In Memoriam

When I met Deborah Sadie Cook at the YMCA we instantly bonded. She was an evangelist and very beautiful. We became great friends and behaved as if we were siblings. I quickly learned that Deborah was not going to let anything or anyone separate her from God. Although she desired a husband she was patiently waiting for God to send her mate. She was faithful until she transitioned in 2016.

I befriended Gwendolyn Mikal Turk at a friend's book release. We talked quite often. Mikal expressed her love for the Lord; her focus was on accomplishing a particular goal. Most important, as a single lady she lived a celibate lifestyle. Mikal was very motivational. She transitioned in March 2017.

Bridgette Truss and I have been friends for about five years. I am arrested by her undying love for the Lord. Bridgett is also waiting patiently and allowing God to position her to receive her husband. I've seen Bridgette grow spiritually. I love her zeal and commitment. I enjoy our daily conversations.

Gloria Jenkins is like a sister. We talk daily and we keep each other grounded. Gloria's commitment to Jehovah is untainted. I admire her strength to remain celibate despite temptations. Gloria truly walks in her faith.

Pastor Glory Fulton is a woman after God's own heart. Glory and I were introduced by a friend. She has a warm heart and loving spirit. Most of all, Glory acknowledges her love for Christ and does not compromise her body for temporary pleasure.

B. Patterson and I have been friends since 2011. She is an amazing woman of God. Her knowledge and love for God is overwhelming. Her love for God will not allow her to sway in the wrong direction. Because of her keen spiritual insight, B., is not challenged by foolishness.

Additionally, she is content being celibate until God sends her husband.

Thanks to Tawonda S. Parker for encouraging and supporting me. Your inspiration was the catalyst in completion of this book.

Tilda and David Love, I have known Tilda for several years, but I have not met her husband David. Tilda is a woman of God who truly loves the Lord. Tilda prayed tirelessly for her husband and God answered her prayers. Furthermore, she was faithful to her commitment to live for God. God showed up and showed out. God blessed Tilda with a man of God. David exemplified his godliness while dating Tilda. Tilda's respect for her husband waxed

strong because he led by example.

ACKNOWLEDGEMENTS

To Amanda Scott, I thank you for your technical support.
Your knowledge and assistance is highly appreciated.

To Eric Cheney, who is a great IT Consultant, I appreciate all the work he has done for me and the time donated to my projects.

To D. Elaine McNease, thank you for being my best friend, sister and editor.

Contents

Preface

I never thought, imagined, or had the slightest idea that I would write relationship books. After all, I was happily married with two children. Then after a few years, things changed in the marriage.

Granted that the union looked good on the outside, there was a struggle in the household and our marriage ended after twenty years; three of those years included separation. I never envisioned being divorced or separated from my children. As a result, I was deeply hurt.

For one reason, my childhood was disheartening because of my parent's separation. Another reason is, knowing that separation or divorce changes the family in so many ways, it was a personal goal to always be in the home with my children.

However, the goal was not reached and there was an adjustment period for the entire family. In fact, while adjusting to this failed marriage a change took place in my life.

In particular, self-examination as a husband, father, and man. Self-examination exposed my weaknesses and short comings. For this reason, the first book, *Am I A Man,* was written. The goal in this book is to help other men look at themselves and become better men; not instructions on being a man.

After the book, *Am I A Man*, and countless failed relationships, I finally found the love I sought. Thus, I met my second wife, Precious Bougrine. Our brief courtship, led to the second book, *Falling In Love God's Way*. What is more, I heard the voice of God say, " I want you to write a book based on falling in love My way." This book entails our surreal relationship and whirlwind courtship.

In my opinion, most people do not allow God's involvement through dictation of principles and guidelines. Of course, God wants people entwined with whom he has chosen. On the contrary, some people follow their own guidelines without any conscious effort to surrender to the one God has chosen. This often leads to failed relationships and marriages.

The intention of *Finding, Receiving, Falling In Love* is to focus on teaching men the different aspects of finding a mate, while aiding women in receiving whom God has ordained for them. The focus is also on different aspects of falling in love.

From my observation, one mistake that many couples make when dating or beginning a relationship is, looking at the outer shell rather than the inner person. In most situations one is naturally attracted to the other

person's physical appearance. It is imperative to know the

person from inside out and not outside in.

Introduction

Finding, Receiving, Falling In Love

As time passes, in this twenty-first century, there are countless failed relationships and marriages. Some are searching for solutions, while many are enduring the hardships of dysfunctional love affairs.

The goal of *Finding, Receiving, Falling In Love* is to point individuals and couples in a positive productive direction. There are viable answers to questions dealing with failing relationships and marriages.

Studies show that the ratio of men to women favor the men. This automatically puts women at a disadvantage and many women become discouraged. On one hand, she is waiting for him to find, romance, and sweep her off her feet.

On the other hand, God is preparing the man as he seeks or finds his mate. In particular, the preparation includes a monogamous relationship.

This can be difficult for some men because of the abundance of choices. When a man is serious he will not frivolously date or pursue a connection. He will wait for God to place him in a position while finding his desired mate. God will also teach him about being the priest of his home.

There are many women who are searching for their mates instead of waiting for the mate. I have heard several women say, "I have to find me a man." However, the word of God says, "Whoso findeth a wife findeth a good thing, and obtaineth favour of the Lord" (Proverbs 18:22 KJV). In essence, the woman should wait for God as He positions her to receive her mate.

Falling in love with Precious, my deceased wife, was a personal plateau. I learned about love in its purest form. It is a surreal feeling knowing when God places one with her or his mate. Indeed, everything fits perfectly.

Although there may be expectations, the love is still unconditional.

Unconditional love is not based on one's status or looks. Furthermore, love speaks from inside out. It is not just spoken, it is also action. Genuine love builds walls that are not penetrated by infidelity or anything negative. True love does exist, but it takes two persons striving daily as they become better individually and collectively.

Finding, Receiving, Falling In Love

Chapter 1 - Falling In Love

Objective or Subjective

Falling in love can be thought of objectively or subjectively. I tend to be more objective when thinking about falling in love. Objective thinkers are neutral, free of bias or prejudice because of personal feelings. Most people have defense mechanisms that do not permit the freedom necessary to engage in a relationship without being bias. Furthermore, their decisions are independent of the mind.

Objectiveness is an indication of unconditional love and one loves another person in spite of; not because of the person's social or economic status. Hence, one is able to dissect the heart of a person. I have learned to positon myself to receive whom God has ordained for me.

Surely, subjective persons base their decisions on opinions or feelings from others. For instance, they tend not to be impartial, but can be one-sided or bias. Subjective lovers are usually conditional lovers. As an illustration, I have been involved in relationships where both parties were subjective. Needless to say, the relationships were temporary.

Nevertheless, whether objective or subjective, being in a relationship is a decision based on one's mindset, situation, or background. Over all, a relationship is based on the choices and desires of each individual. Most of all, a couple should mutually agree without one coercing the other.

As an example, a potential mate wanted to get an understanding of our relationship status. Therefore, she requested a meeting. The meeting went well and we were able to discuss our goals, desires, and feelings. She had aspirations for an exclusive relationship, while I was not ready to commit.

Although it is not a good idea to expedite a relationship prematurely; it is always good to know that both parties are in agreement. There are many situations where one person's desires are different than their counterpart's.

In some cases, there are those who try to force their will on others. In most instances these relationships are unhealthy and futile.

Due to pressure from family and friends some people feel compelled to either remain or refrain from a relationship. More importantly, another person's opinion should not determine factors in a couple's relationship.

Certainly, one can receive opinions without biases. However, a couple should make decisions without interference from family and friends.

Given that a decision is a process of reaching a conclusion, it is important to make choices and decisions based on cogent factors such as, character and intellect. As a matter of fact, many potential relationships are affected negatively as a result of status quo type advice.

When one has a status quo mindset, it is difficult to look beyond a person's status. For instance, a status quo mind set is captivated by things such as, the type of car a person drives, income level, social status, type of home, or wardrobe.

Besides, there are countless relationships that never develop because some people are misjudged due to their social and economic status. Some people may feel that they cannot measure up to the expectation of others. For this reason, it is difficult to make decisions with outside interference.

A couple can be influenced by outside interference when making a decision on whether to be or not to be (in a relationship). Now, some couples make the decision of not being in a relationship. Of course, this could be temporary or long term. In fact, pausing or taking a break from the rigors of a relationship is beneficial. For one thing, it can be a time of contentment and self-examination; yet another, growth or sabbatical.

In summary, the status of a couple's relationship is determined by both parties. For this reason, a decision is made based on their standards.

Another example of a relationship decision is, self-examination. A friend was asked why he was not dating a certain young lady; he responded, "I am working on me, although she is a good woman, I am not where I need to be." As previously stated, this was done in my failed marriage situation. Recognizing the need for self-examination is important.

Lisa Villa Prosen, an accomplished author and speaker, stated "The happiest people I know are always evaluating and improving themselves. The unhappy people are usually evaluating and judging others." Especially, people who are in abusive and unproductive relationships.

An abusive or unproductive relationship is the reason some people hesitate when yielding to another. No doubt, pain, disappointment, mistreatment, and neglect build walls, which becomes a fortress that says, "No" to love.

Due to horrific experiences, some relationships suffer with up-setting emotions. As a result, this suffering affects decision making. Consequently, one may hesitate when entering a new relationship.

When one suffers, and endures the hardships of a disheartening relationship it provokes a sense of precaution and patience. Furthermore, one becomes hesitant when expressing feelings or emotions.

Therefore, a wall comes up and the person will not divulge much personal information. Because of this, a communication problem may arise. It is gratifying when a person openly communicates, which signifies a heighten trust. So many relationships are stagnated because of "ghost" of the past.

When a person's wall is up, she or he needs understanding and tolerance in the relationship. Assuredly, the person with the wall up is saying, "I am not comfortable or ready to expedite detailed information." Over all, an effective solution for bringing and keeping the wall down is patience.

Move Beyond The Past

Those who are aware of my relationship pitfalls; especially, my failed first marriage, would not believe that I am so open to give and receive love.

As a reflection, I met my first wife during my last year in college. She was walking in the parking lot with a young lady and my classmate. I immediately asked my classmate, "Who is the friend that is walking with you?"

All who knows me will readily tell you that I am not shy when it comes to approaching a female. After a brief introduction, we talked and exchanged numbers.

I was highly intrigued by this intelligent and beautiful woman. She attended Georgia State University and was a native of Atlanta. I had no idea that I would be captivated to the extent of falling in love with her. Finally, after dating for about a year and a half we married.

As mentioned earlier, our marriage lasted twenty years on paper. The first few years were captivating and exciting. I must admit, I was not ready for marriage nor did I truly understand the magnitude of being in a relationship. I was in love, but did not understand how to walk in love.

In addition, my love was more dependent on emotions and physical feelings. Thus, knowing love from a carnal aspect and not from a spiritual realm. I did not understand the importance of being foundationally sound in a Godly way. No doubt, I had not learned to apply the word of God in my marital life.

Instead of accepting confusion, disagreement, and disharmony as a norm in marriage, there should have been rebuking, binding, and loosing those interfering spirits from Satan.

I now recognize that Satan hates holy matrimony and tries to destroy marriages. It is of the utmost importance that couples are joined at the hip in prayer and meditation.

Love is more than just saying, "I love you" or having a physical encounter. Furthermore, one should not confuse love with lust or sexual escapades. Besides, a climax is quick, but love is intensive and eternal.

Love speaks through a person's attitude, actions, and character. Love is more than just an emotion or verbal outcry; it looks into the heart of a person. Love also responds through character, morals, and visions.

My ineptness contributed to a disastrous end in marriage. I was a terrible husband and did not know how to walk in the role of a priest or head of home. Ultimately, she said, "I have fallen out of love with you."

I have often heard people say, "I fell out of love with my mate." One may wonder if the person was truly in love, or can a person's mishaps or negative demeanor cause one's love to diminish.

If a mate has endured their spouse's incompetent actions for a lengthy period it initiates discontentment. Often times effective counseling will help differentiate falling out of love, being unhappy, or unfulfilled.

Many times, as a result of counseling, one will recognize the deficiencies. For this reason, the marriage is transformed.

I made the mistake of not receiving counseling, which could have saved my failed marriage. However, I did ask God to help me become a better man and husband. Unfortunately, my request was made during the period we were separated. God granted my request and I became a better man, but it was too late to salvage the marriage.

Even before meeting my ex-wife, there was a previous pit fall relationship. This relationship lasted about three years and ended abruptly. She was a good woman and we had a good relationship. Our greatest problem was the result of my discrepancies or indiscretions.

During that time, I was a terrible mate, a Morehouse College student, who stayed on campus with Spellman, Clark, and Morris Brown Colleges within close proximity. Reflecting on my college days, dating was something that I did frivolously.

Always One That Got Away

Upon maturation and several failed relationships, I realize that "she" was the one that got away. I actually began dating or became interested in a young lady who attended Spellman College. Although, I was in love with her, this new relationship never really escalated to my expectations.

Ironically, I always regretted not marrying her. As a matter of fact, I never stop loving her. I had not met a woman with the same calm demeanor until I met Precious (my second wife). The young lady and I went out for several months and I saw her interact in adverse situations. What is more, she always maintained the same serenity.

We maintained a friendship after college and she went to graduate school in New York and I went to play Minor League Baseball in Florida.

Don't Let Her Get Away

Consider this, most men have one special woman that in hindsight is thought of as the one who got away. For instance, a friend William, stated, "I did not pay attention to her needs, did not listen, and stopped doing the things I did to get her. Now I regret it because she got away."

When choosing a female companion, some men overlook viable candidates for possible matrimony because of unlimited options. For this reason, one can lose the appreciation for a virtuous woman. It is unmerited when a woman of substance is devalued. When a man does not appreciate the love, kindness, and support from his mate it diminishes her worth. Another friend, Keisha G., stated, "A woman of essence adds to a man's well-being and not subtracts."

Love In Its Purest Form

Falling in love can be a wonderful experience. Once a person encounters love in its purest form she or he becomes addicted to being genuinely and unconditionally loved.

There are no fears, vulnerabilities, indiscretions, and no reason for being precautious. Further, there is a feeling of completeness and total fulfillment. Without a doubt, it seems surreal. Experiencing pure and genuine love is a valuable experience in my life. This unique time happened after Precious and I married.

This marriage lasted only four months. Precious went home to be with her Lord! Although this was a brief period it was extraordinary. We encountered various occurrences which seems like forty years.

I often wish for one more day of life with Precious; one day would seem like a thousand years. I would love seeing Precious' beautiful smile, visualizing her captivating countenance, and hearing say, "I love you honey."

There is a special feeling when one is loved unconditionally. Precious said, that I was "God's gift to her," and I know that she was God's gift to me. I thank God for having the opportunity to experience pure love for a few months as opposed to never having the opportunity.

Our love reflected something I read, "Find a love not like others, find a love that speaks to you, a love that speaks from you." I advise everyone to do the same when seeking love.

I realize that everyone could not have been married to Precious, neither could everyone be married to me. Surely, we were entwined, and we were each other's supposed to be. Furthermore, we looked at each other through God's eyes, and we knew we had an uphill battle because marriage is working each day to maintain oneness.

In the book, *Falling In Love God's Way*; I admonish others not to give up. In Chapter 7 the topic is, Don't Stop Climbing The Mountain. There are several suggestions in this chapter on climbing the mountain of marriage.

In particular, "When climbing the mountain of marriage one must realize that the higher the couple climbs, it seems that they will have even higher to go. The motivating factor is progression and not digression." There is also a suggestion to "have backpacks" when climbing the mountain of marriage.

The backpacks will consist of aids that will assist the couple when there is a deficiency in their marriage. These aids could be godliness, patience, compassion, forgiveness and more. Marriage is work and thinking that it is not is a deception. This is why having the back pack available makes the work easier.

Love Traps

Unfortunately, many people do not experience love in an unadulterated way. Often times, a love trap is the reason for getting involved in a situation that is difficult to get out of. There are several reasons. For one, it could be bonding with the wrong mate or settling for someone unnecessarily. And then another, may be getting involved because of deception.

Love traps can be dangerous. Especially, when one sacrifices feelings unequally. In fact, taking advantage of one's feelings is travesty. Surely, expressing love to someone when love does not exist is a love trap. Indeed, this is taking advantage of that person's feelings.

Love traps are situations in a relationship that are misleading, confining, controlling, promiscuous, or unhealthy.

I believe that, one of the most interesting love traps in the Bible is, Jacob falling in love with Rachelle (Genesis 29:10-30) and asking her father, Laban, for permission to marry her; Laban gave Jacob permission to marry Rachel. However, he was deceived into marrying Leah, Laban's oldest daughter. Jacob's desire to marry Rachel was so immense that he allowed Laban to manipulate and mislead him. Jacob was in a love trap because he ended up marrying Leah, and after seven years he married Rachel. Therefore, he ended up with two wives, which later caused much confusion.

Another example of an entrapment or love trap is, the movie, *Soldier's Girl*. This movie was based on a true story about a soldier (Barry Mitchell) who falls in love with a transgender (Calpernia Addams). The soldier began frequenting a gay club and became attracted to the transgender.

Barry was initially captivated by the personality of Calpernia; despite the fact that her role at birth was male gender. In other words, the transgender person was transsexual. Calpernia continually asked Barry if he knew what he was getting into. As time passed Barry did not care what anyone thought. Although some people thought that he was gay, he did not consider himself gay. Barry just thought of himself as being in love. He was trapped with his own emotions.

There are so many homosexual, heterosexual, and transsexual relationships that have resulted in love traps. Many are lured into a love trap and get stuck in it. The irony is no matter whom one dates whether heterosexual, homosexual, or transsexual the same issues may arise in the relationship.

Do Not Be Anxious Be Prayerful

Many love trap situations are avoidable. In particular, as recommended in the book, *Falling In Love God's Way*, being prayerful before entering a relationship is helpful.

It is difficult for many people to receive whom God has ordained for them; mainly because most people do not seek spiritual guidance when making decisions.

Additionally, most people strive for connection with whom they desire, or who may want them.

When relationships are ordained by God there is impenetrable equilibrium. Countless relationships fail due to a lack of prayer and guidance, which leads to a lack of symmetry.

Regardless of gender there will always be someone who wants to get involved interpersonally. What is more, it will be glaringly obvious when there is an imbalance. Indeed, one person may desire or expect more than the other is willing to give. Therefore, the relationship will end.

Being anxious is one reason that the relationship is prematurely expedited. Another reason is, Lack of prayer, and failed expectations. As a case in point, if a person does not receive what she or he gives, this will cause discontentment and discord.

Seen One You Have Seen Them All

At one point in my life, I was enamored by the physical beauty of a woman. No doubt, the possession of a lustful spirit was involved.

My judgment would initially be outside in and not inside out. To my dismay many times the chemistry would be lacking, especially mentally.

It is one thing being attracted to the natural beauty of a woman, yet another is, realizing that seeing one is seeing them all. Whereas, this does not mean becoming oblivious. Of course, it is refreshing to compliment a woman unassumingly or innocently. For instance, it is good to say, "You look nice today," "You are beautiful," or "Your hair is nice."

At my present place of employment, I screen each person as they enter the workout facility. I often hear guys say, "I would love to have your job because you get to see all the pretty women." Personally, I am not overwhelmed as most people might be.

More importantly, my hormones are in a controlled state. In any event, it is a pleasure learning to appreciate the wholeness of a woman; her soul, spirit and body.

Do Not Seek Your Soul Mate

Many people are looking for their soul mate and end up with a stalemate. Being a soul mate is a connection in the flesh. The soul is a person's mind, will, and emotions. This is discussed later in more detail.

According to the Encarta Dictionary, the definition of stalemate is, "A situation with no potential winners or to put somebody or something into a situation in which no further worthwhile action is possible."

How many times have you felt that you found your soulmate? In a like manner, there is seemingly a connection with each other in a special way.

Suddenly, there is a disconnection such as, arguing, fussing, and fighting. Next, the relationship seems like a rollercoaster, but you keep trying to hold on. Consequently, your soulmate has become your stalemate!

Therefore, the relationship abruptly ends or you continue to hold on to your mate despite the discord. Moreover, when meeting in a fleshly realm at some point there has to be transference to the spiritual realm. The transference to the spiritual realm is the foundation of a Godly relationship.

A relationship that has a spiritual foundation will survive the hindrances and frustrations that the flesh presents. When a couple is on a spiritual plane, it is easier to stay connected.

Even if they are disengaged by disagreements or personal differences, being on one accord spiritually will bring prayer instead of strife, patience, not intolerance, and forgiveness not un-forgiveness.

I enjoy telling my story of saying to Precious, "I have found my best friend, soul mate, and wife." She quickly responded, "Honey I am not your soul mate I am your spirit mate!"

Yes, I was confused, but after prayer the Holy Spirit said to me, "When you are connected in the soul you are connected in the flesh; the mind, will, and emotions, but when you are connected in the spirit you are connected directly to me."

I then recognized that many relationships fail

because of soul connections. When connected in the flesh

and disagreements occur they are mostly dealt with by

fussing and fighting. When connected in the spirit the

couple will pray jointly or independently.

Chapter 2 - Finding Your Mate

There are some important factors incorporated in a man finding his mate. First, he should not be unequally yoked. In biblical days farmers yoked animals together to plow fields and carry heavy loads.

These animals were paired off and had a piece of wood, which connected them together. This enabled them to perform a task more easily. For example, horses, oxen, donkeys, and mules paired in this fashion pulled loads and plowed fields. As a case in point, they were equally yoked to get the job done.

Second, it is important realizing that it is the man's responsibility to find his mate, girlfriend, or wife. Therefore, he must find a mate to share the relationship load.

Certainly, both of them will bear the load of maintaining the relationship. Especially, being equally yoked. Being equally yoked is a reminder of the biblical example in a previous paragraph.

Although there are many who do not adhere to biblical principles the Scripture states, "Whoso findeth a wife findeth a good thing and obtaineth favour of the Lord" (Proverbs 18:22, KJV).

Regardless of one's belief it is a good protocol to follow. Of course, there are some who would venture to dispute this thought. In fact, it is thought by some people that, it is all right for a woman to find her man or mate.

Many people also believe that, when a woman chases a man it appears that she is impatient, loose, or easy. Most men with genuine intentions like to hunt and not be hunted.

It is all right for a woman to express interest or reciprocate advances from a desired suitor, but she should always be his greatest challenge.

There are times when some women allow their emotions to expedite their feelings. This causes premature interaction with a potential suitor. From my point of view, couples should avoid a first date kiss and sexual encounters; as some make think this is the "norm."

That type of situation usually determines if one is ordinary or extraordinary. Most men who are genuinely seeking wives are enamored when the women they are interested in are unique. Some people hold the opinion that an easy woman can be considered ordinary, but a virtuous woman is extraordinary.

Eve was presented to Adam; God said it was not good for man to be alone. Adam was waiting for Eve; not Eve waiting for Adam. Of course, Eve was formed from Adam's rib. When God said, "It is not good for man to be alone," all Adam had to do was wait for his wife.

Often times a man will get impatient when seeking his mate. Impatience brings about overreaction when meeting a desired mate. Thus, over reaction leads one to expedite the relationship prematurely. It is imperative for the man not to treat a girl friend as he would a wife. What is more, the couple should stay in a friendship relationship for a period of time before moving to the dating stage.

Approach

In the Bible Isaac found Rebekka, Boaz found Ruth in the grain field. Isaac and Boaz followed proper protocol when pursuing their mates. In this day and time, it seems that many men cannot connect with the women they are pursuing because they do not approach them properly.

Indeed, using proper ice breakers is essential when the initial contact is made. Ice breakers are simply the approach used to start a conversation or to get someone's attention.

When approaching a possible suitor one must not be afraid. Fear often occurs when the possible suitor seems unapproachable, unusually appealing, or is affluent. I feel

that there are many men who allow a woman's tentative

demeanor to cause fear or hesitancy. A woman may seem

unapproachable because of a negative experience or just

not dating.

I suppose, when a woman has a wall up her

emotional state of mind can be very low. She then can be

unreceptive to advances from men. Her mindset is focused

on her personal well-being, and not being in a relationship.

It is seemingly difficult to connect with women who

are highly attractive. Surely, It has been my experience that

women whom I consider highly attractive are very

approachable. Again, the most important thing is not to be timid or tentative.

From my experience, an affluent woman may be the most difficult to approach because she usually desires a mate that is her equal. My approach to all types of women is very simple. First, I establish eye contact. Next, when no eye contact is established I initiate a non-threatening conversation. For instance, I will say things like, "how are you?" "It's a nice day," "I like your hair," or other complementary topics.

Greetings such as, "Hey baby," "What's up beautiful," or "Hey slim," must be eliminated from your introduction. Of course, first impressions must be positive and non-threatening.

Conversation

Having the proper approach is a must, but the right approach must be followed by a mature sensible conversation.

It goes without saying, one major complaint that some women have is, many men do not know how to verbally communicate. Some men have the perfect approach and have no problem asking for a desired phone number. However, the problem often occurs because the communication is ineffective. The man who communicates effectively with his mate will pave a smooth road to a

successful relationship. Dialogue is simply having a

conversation between two or more people. Men in general

have been labeled as non-communicative. Women often

complain about how difficult it is to discuss certain issues

with men. Some women have been labeled as

argumentative, crabby, complainers, or short tempered.

Men are often labeled as precarious. In other words,

sometimes dangerously insecure or unsettled in opinion.

There are certain do's and don'ts that must be

adhered to in the initial stages of the friendship. The

conversation should be more formal than informal unless

otherwise agreed upon. Over all, the conversation should just naturally flow, and recognizing what is acceptable will automatically surface. After all, finding the right words to say is not difficult when one genuinely desires to know another person from within.

It is not proper to invite yourself to a woman's home on your first meeting. I have had several encounters where I was not allowed in a home visit for one to three months. It is also improper to invite her to your home in the early stages of the friendship.

A Connection

When a man is searching for his mate or a woman is waiting for her beau the first stage of any relationship is the connection. Additionally, the most important aspect of a man connecting with a woman is praying and asking God to send and reveal the woman He has ordained for the man.

When seeking God for a divine connection, the man is establishing a spiritual base in the relationship. Likewise, God is joining the union. Therefore, it is not solely dependent on the man making a personal decision.

Of course, when two people have prayed, and received confirmation that they are each other's "Supposed To Be," as mentioned in the book, *Falling In Love God's Way*, a divine connection is made. This eliminates marrying the wrong person, which often ends in divorce or broken homes.

A connection signifies chemistry, a bond, or oneness. This is the first sign of commonality. There is no greater feeling than having harmony, camaraderie, or shared goals when a person meets and bonds with a mate.

As a case in point, when a couple has common interest, it allows the dating process to flow fluently. In the connection stage, being patient allows the relationship to develop properly. What is more, being connected to God is what I call, "being entwined." As a result, a firm foundation is established.

It is important that the connection is not just one person feeling connected and the other person not fully connected. Many times, a man will tell a woman, "You are going to be my wife." I have heard a lot of women say, "I don't know why he's calling me his wife, I am not feeling it!" I can imagine, this gives many women uncomfortable and annoying feelings.

Men are hunters or seekers and it is natural feeling connected when finding someone who is seemingly overwhelming. Again, the key is allowing the relationship to develop properly. Men have a tendency to be impatient, spontaneous, and abrupt. As mentioned earlier it is advantageous that both parties are connected spiritually.

Most relationships are initially connected in the flesh. Fleshly connections are finite and dependent on superficial conditions. The late Maya Angelou, an American Poet, memoirist, and civil rights activist, stated, "A woman's heart should be hidden in God that a man has to seek Him just to find her."

How To Connect

I would say that, there are vast amount of men who are not dating or have not found the mate they desire. I often remind myself that I may not find the perfect mate, but she will be perfect for me.

Given that this has worked for me, I advise others to connect by seeking spirit, mind, and body. Most men are visual and seek their mates in the reverse order, body, mind, and spirit.

We, as men, usually connect with the posterior, breast, hair, or total body shape. Exterior attraction can be over rated and short lived. Especially, if the attraction diminishes. Personally, I look into the heart of the woman, then I see if her lifestyle reflects what her heart and mind speaks.

Finally, I appreciate her outer beauty to a greater extent, but it is not my main focus. Every man will have his likes and dislikes. Nevertheless, it is more important to have a godly connection.

Pray To Receive Her

The basis of pursuing a mate is, precede with prayer. At the same time, one should also use wisdom. Significantly, a prayer of consecration or blessing upon the desired union. Praying for discernment about the woman God sends is crucial. Above all, be specific about your desires.

A friend told me that he prayed for the qualities that he wanted in his wife. I asked what they were. He said, "I prayed that she was a woman of God, that she was not moody, and that she was pleasing to his eyes."

Given that there is so much deception in the dating arena in this day and time, discernment is necessary to avoid all the dating schemes and scams. My prayer when interested in a woman is that God reveals her heart. I have met women who were concerned about my financial status and desired a man financially stable. There is nothing wrong with that, but it becomes erroneous when one's feelings are dictated by money. When a woman's heart is pure, the man she desires may not possess a feasible bank account, but he may have other dominant attributes. While praying to receive a mate, the man must determine if she's genuinely interested or if it is a free date or meal. I have dated women who were just free dates, they would go on the date, but were not truly interested in a long-term relationship.

Praying for a mate keeps one in a place of contentment and personal happiness. This means that a person is prepared to meet the mate with assurance and confidence. Furthermore, after this there is no room for anxiety.

Once God presents a man with his mate, there is an urgency for prayer. Pray for her; in addition, if the opportunity presents itself pray with her.

Satan is against anything that represents oneness, righteousness, and godliness. He does not want a person to pray for or with a potential mate.

She must accept you

There may come a time when a man meets a woman and it seems obvious that this is the woman that he desires as his wife. On the contrary, the connection is not complete until he is accepted as her beau.

For example, I excitedly found someone who met the character traits of the woman I desired as a wife. We seemed to instantly bond. Moreover, our ministries complimented each other and I could see us easily going to another level as marriage and ministry partners.

I learned from this experience that it is crucial for the man to not just pray for his prospective mate, but pray with her also. As mentioned earlier, this is an urgency.

Needless to say, although I was very transparent she changed her concept about detrimental issues we discussed concerning our possible union.

I was confused, but then realized that if she had recognized that I was her gift from God, her doubts and fears would have been eliminated.

At the time my finances were low and her expectation was for her husband to have a certain income level. This was totally contradictory to an extensive conversation we discussed about financial status. Thus, I realized she was not the one God had ordained for me. I was not considered her gift from God.

How will she know?

Finding a mate or love can be difficult. Surely, it is rewarding when found. In fact, a man must distinguish the type of mate he is searching for.

Men, I venture to ask, "What are you searching for or what type of woman are you desiring?" As for me the search is for my spirit mate, meaning a woman who connects with me spiritually. She will know me by divine revelation.

There will not be any doubt that we are connected by God. When I have an interest in a potential mate I always ask her to seek God about my purpose in her life.

A woman who has prayed and received confirmation will recognize her gift from God. Thus, when a relationship is consummated through prayer and confirmed by the Holy Spirit a spiritual foundation is laid.

Otherwise, when a woman places her assurance on superficial feelings or reasons this is not a spiritual foundation. In this particular situation, everything seems so right. Of course, the chemistry is seemingly there; the man is saying and doing all the right things.

Although, the couple connected physically, occupationally, and socially there may be questions as to why the relationship fizzled. Especially, after a short period of time. Granted, everything seems cohesive but is dysfunctional. For this reason, the couple is disengaged spiritually.

All in all, there are many relationships that do not evolve spiritually they are fulfilled temporarily in a carnal state. The two must be spiritually compatible.

Basic Needs For Women

A relationship or marriage needs proper nurturing with sincere intentions. It is imperative that a man understands the basic needs of a woman and the needs will vary based on individual prerequisites.

Open communication is necessary because it aids in the connecting of hearts. Most women like expressing their feelings while men have a tendency to wear their emotions on their sleeves.

There is a special bond when mates are able to discuss problems, challenges, and goals while accepting each other's shortcomings. It is vital making a conscious effort to improve the areas of concern.

Women appreciate having mates who listen to their concerns or issues. No doubt, positive communication is necessary to cultivate a relationship.

Many people believe that most women's prerequisite is the financial security that a man offers. There are many women whose need exceeds the amount of money the man has or earn.

During my first marriage, my wife was not as concerned about my finances as she was about my ability to make sure the needs were orchestrated properly. It was important to her that I contacted the Plummer, landscaper, or mechanic to set the appointments. The issue was not money, but just supporting her in an organizational aspect.

Security

Security is a major concern for most women. When a woman feels secure her mate or husband becomes her fortress. Likewise, most women want to feel safe financially, have a secure relationship, and a man of strength. Every situation is different and a man should do what is necessary to make his situation viable.

Besides that, he must not be weak in character or easily controlled. No doubt, emotional toughness, sound morals, and being trustworthy breeds a sense of security. On the whole, a man's strength should exceed his financial status.

Leadership

As a good leader, a husband is not controlling or abusive. He leads by overseeing, protecting, and providing the necessities of the household. One man's strength may be another man's weakness. As an example, some men are excellent at repairing things, landscaping, car repairs while others are good at cooking, housekeeping, and bookkeeping. In many situations, the most important factor is, as a leader, the man should make sure that the job is accomplished.

Income status should not dictate leadership. A man can earn considerably less than his wife, and still be the leader or head of household. There are many situations where the man of the house feels subordinate to his spouse due to lack of income. In many situations, the wife becomes domineering.

However, a woman will surrender her authority to a man she respects. There are situations where the woman has an authoritative position at work, but prefer being in a lessor role at home.

It is imperative that a man takes his rightful place as priest of his home. This does not mean he becomes a dictator or bossy. As a matter of fact, he simply walks in his God given authority. As a result, his wife or mate will openly dialogue and seek her mate's or husband's advice.

I have counseled women who were frustrated because their husbands were bossy and domineering. Additionally, other complaints were, their spouses "always had the last word." Surely, Self-righteous attitudes are recipes for failure or divorce.

Sensitivity

Most women are keen on sensitivity. For instance, they are sensitive in areas that men take for granted. A woman wants to feel that her mate is hearing and listening to her concerns.

There is a difference between hearing and listening. We, as people, often hear but do not listen. On one hand, effective listening is understanding what another person saying. On the other hand, listening involves paying attention or making a conscious effort to hear.

The two are interchangeable; one cannot listen without hearing or hear without listening. As men, being sensitive to a woman's needs is essential. Therefore, a man must not take his mate for granted. For one thing, he should recognize the importance of hearing. Yet another is, responding properly and addressing certain areas of concern in a positive manner.

Non-sexual commitment

Most men think of women as having the candy store. The candy store for most men is the motivating factor of being involved in a relationship. Men usually look for sex while women seek commitment.

Virtuous women appreciate non-sexual obligations. A major complaint that I receive from women is, men making sex the main topic of initial conversations.

This can be a major turn off. Furthermore, appreciating the beauty of a woman from inside out is crucial. Consequently, her true identity is exposed. This is the result of examining her heart. The representation of that woman is revealed through her character. A person's moral fiber should be the root of her or his attraction.

Unconditional Love

Unconditional love is a powerful attribute. In essence, a person is expressing provision for complete submission, without limitations for the feelings of another person. For this reason, it is critical for a man to seek a woman who will love him unconditionally; as he loves her in the same way. In particular, she must recognize that he is the man for her based on whom God sent; not the man's status.

This allows one to love from the inside out. Moreover, one can see the mate as God sees that person. *As stated in Falling in Love God's Way,* "A feeling of love for most people is definitely conditional and is usually

based on some type of prerequisite. In other words, some

people say, "I love you because…" We could fill in the

blank with, "what you have, "how you look," "how you

make me feel," or "who you are." Furthermore, this

establishes the need for unconditional love.

Chose and Not Be Chosen

There are numerous women who make the mistake

of choosing their mate. There is a distinct difference in

choosing and being chosen.

For instance, when a woman makes a deliberate decision to initiate a relationship with a man, she is in danger of being in a volatile situation or relationship.

First, the man becomes the receiver; he is now in the position of his female counterpart. Second, she is the hunter; hunting is the man's position. Third, the woman could become vulnerable because her defense mechanisms are lessened.

A friend, Keith, and I were discussing relationships; as we talked he made a powerful statement, "Men must choose to be chosen." There are many men who are not available because of choosing not to make a monogamous commitment.

In essence, the man who is dating to marry is not waiting to be chosen, but makes it known that he does the choosing and is prepared to seek his mate.

As men, we choose the woman that we desire, but ultimately the woman has to decide if she wants to proceed in a friendship or relationship. It is of the utmost importance that the man recognizes the person God presents to him. Being men, we must avoid interference at all cost, and not allow it from anyone. Most important, when God ordains the relationship, interference is definitely not allowed.

I often hear people say, "God will give you the desires of your heart." I believe that He will and does when people live according to God's Word. In contrast, sometimes our desires exceed what God desires for us.

Checklist / Red Flags

Men must understand that many women will not approve the bonding of a relationship if something is missing on her checklist.

Check lists vary from income status, appearance, hygiene, morals, to character.

Red flags are issues that can deter or hinder someone. As a matter of fact, overlooking them can lead to a disastrous relationship. Red flags also represent the negative aspect of a person's character.

Minimizing each red flag to its lowest common denominator is essential. As an example, a negative attitude, an annoyance, or a bad habit. This will help one decide if this is the person God chose for her or him.

The most important aspect of a red flag is resolution. As a case in point, if the situation is not resolved, can the offending person tolerate it without causing division, frustration, anger, or hostility? If not, then it is best not to continue the relationship. Usually, people do not change. What is more, if there is a transformation it takes hard work over an extended period of time. One must recognize the shortcomings and have an earnest desire to improve.

If the relationship is entwined by God and there are some red flags that are questionable, God will make provisions for the union. The key is being sure that God approves the union.

Next, God will give the person wisdom and patience necessary to tolerate unpleasant habits. Always remember when God is the foundation of a union He provides and seals any deficiencies, doubts, and fears.

Notable Red Flags

Notable red flags differ from person to person. What might be an issue for one may not be an issue for another.

Some Red Flags That Could Get Men's Attention

1. She has children and you either already have children or you do not want to raise another person's child or children.

2. She is seemingly overly indigent. Whereas, you might be accustomed to an independent low maintenance type of woman.

3. Overly cantankerous or grouchy, gets angry easily, controversial, or difficult to get along with.

4. Too Controlling, being in charge, and things must go her way.

Whatever notable red flags exists they must be resolved or it could damage the growth of the union.

He Not She That Finds

According to the Word of God, Women who think they have to find their men are totally out of order. It does not say anything about a woman finding a man. As previously quoted, "Whoso findeth a wife findeth a good thing..." (Proverbs 18:22). It is natural for a man to seek his mate. The most important factor is finding the woman that God has prepared for him. This can only happen as a result of prayer and patience. After this, the man will seek that unique and extraordinary woman who will challenge him to live a life of godliness.

Chapter 3 - Receiving Your Mate

Looking at Ephesians 5:23, "The husband is the head of the wife as Christ is the head of the church." Headship is leadership, sacrifice, love, and obedience. God did not intend for man to rule, control, or dominate his wife, but lead and protect her.

Of course, the man must make the necessary sacrifices in every area to fulfill the sanctity of the union. Each situation is different and is handled accordingly. In the Scripture, husbands are exhorted to "Love their wives, as Christ loved the church and gave himself for her"

(Ephesians 5:25). When a husband loves his wife, he sacrifices his life for her and their family.

The two are harmonious because they are in agreement with God and each other. Without a doubt, Christ is the head of the union.

A husband who is a provider is a giver. He should give of himself financially, as well as his time and unconditional love. He may not be the sole provider, but at least a contributor, if agreed upon by his spouse.

As a sustainer, the husband gives moral support and upholds the wife when she needs a shoulder to lean on. All in all, when a man protects his mate she feels secure in knowing that she is covered by his presence.

An interesting post on Facebook, "Subject: SELF WORTH (Very Deep!!!). In a brief conversation, a man questioned a woman he was pursuing: What kind of man are you looking for? She sat quietly for a moment before looking him in the eye & asking, do you really want to know? Reluctantly, he said, Yes. She began to expound, As a woman in this day & age, I am in a position to ask a man what can you do for me that I can't do for myself? I pay my own bills. I take care of my household without the help of any man... or woman for that matter. I am in the position to ask, What can you bring to the table? The man looked at her. Clearly, he thought that she was referring to money. She quickly corrected his thought & stated, I am not referring to money. I need something more. I need a man who is striving for excellence in every aspect of life. He sat back in his chair, folded his arms, & asked her to explain. She said, I need someone who is striving for excellence mentally because I need conversation & mental stimulation. I don't need a simple-minded man. I need someone who is striving for excellence spiritually because I don't need to be unequally yoked...believers mixed with unbelievers is a recipe for disaster. I need a man who is striving for excellence financially because I don't need a financial burden. I need someone who is sensitive enough to understand what I go through as a woman, but strong enough to keep me grounded. I need someone who has integrity in dealing with relationships. Lies and game-playing are not my idea of a strong man. I need a man who is family-oriented. One who can be the leader, priest and provider to the lives entrusted to him by God. I need someone whom I can respect. In order to be submissive, I must respect him. I cannot be submissive to a man who isn't taking care of his business. I have no problem being submissive...he just has to be worthy. And by the way, I am not looking for him...He will find me. He will recognize

himself in me. Hey may not be able to explain the

connection, but he will always be drawn to me. God made

woman to be a helpmate for man. I can't help a man if he

can't help himself. When she finished her spill, she looked

at him. He sat there with a puzzled look on his face. He

said, 'You are asking a lot. She replied, I'm worth a lot.

Send this to every woman who's worth a lot.... and every

man who has the brains to understand!!!"

I applaud the woman who wrote this and encourage

every female to use it as a guideline. The most important

advice I would give any woman desiring to receive her beau, mate, or husband is, be patient and prayerful.

When a woman does not have the fortitude to endure singleness, loneliness, or celibacy she may abruptly and dialogically begin to search for her desired mate.

Hunters naturally try to gain an advantage on prey. When fishing I often times use bait spray on my lure to attract the fish. They will smell the odor and attack the bait. This is my deceptive way of catching more fish. There are times the fish will spit the artificial lure out. When the fish recognize deception they immediately rectify and protect themselves from being captured.

My advice to women is, display the same demeanor when detecting misleading behavior. It is imperative in being discerning when evaluating the man's character.

A woman should not be influenced by a man's finances, appearance, or social status. Just as fish recognize deception and disengage from every indication of dishonesty women should do the same.

Do Not Be Violated

Most women are alert as to how men approach them; as some women put it, "Seeing what type of game he has." It is a tactic for some men to identify a woman's weakness then proceed to violate her.

Weaknesses in women vary, but is easily detected by an observant man. One of the greatest weaknesses displayed by some women is having low self-esteem.

One of the glaring traits of low self-esteem is being overly dependent, which causes vulnerability and neediness.

For example, some women feel incomplete without men in their lives. Moreover, in some cases they become dependent on his presence or dominance.

Furthermore, this sense of neediness often times leads to disrespect which violates the woman.

Be Virtuous

Abstinence is one way of being extraordinary. A mature man will be more open to a woman who abstained from sex rather than a promiscuous woman.

In essence, she is recognized as being extraordinary and not ordinary. Therefore, the man categorizes her as a woman of virtue. Having good virtues means she will have desirable qualities.

While thinking about a woman having virtue, the Proverbs 31 woman comes to mind. In this Proverb, the question is asked, "Who can find a virtuous woman?" The word "virtuous" has a powerful meaning.

Virtuous is described with several interpretations in the Bible. The New International Version (NIV) states, "A wife of noble character." She is simply a woman of high moral principles and ideas. Gentleness is also a virtuous woman trait. The English Standard Version (ESV) describes the virtuous woman as being excellent. "An excellent wife who can find? "

The synonyms for excellent are, very good, superb, outstanding, exceptional, marvelous, and wonderful. A woman who possesses any of these qualities is highly desired.

The International Standard Version (ISV) says, "Who can find a capable wife?" The synonyms for capable are also captivating. They are, have the ability to, be equal to (the task of), be up to, have what it takes to (be).

When a woman possesses the qualities listed above this automatically makes her extraordinary and desirable. Potential suitors seek women who are unique and mature. These women are what most men call keepers.

Be Complete

An extraordinary woman will have a charisma that says, "I am complete." The Encarta Dictionary defines charisma as, "A personal magnetism, the ability to inspire enthusiasm, interest, or affection in others by means of personal charm or influence."

Completeness is termed as not being dependent or needy. Most men desire a woman who is independent. She stands out like a sore thumb. In fact, her dependence is voluntary and is chosen at the proper time. Similarly, her independence will not allow her to be controlled nor will she try to control her mate. She will love him and respect his love for her.

Be A Challenge

Women who are seeking a divine and eternal relationship should strive to be the greatest challenge that a man has experienced. As previously stated, "she must be extraordinary not ordinary."

Most relationships involve premarital sex, which is a common place among those who begin dating. Most men will respect a woman who is not promiscuous and has defined boundaries.

I advise women to openly discuss their position on dating and marriage. Ultimately, the relationship is tested when emotions are heightened. If a desired mate does not want to adhere to being abstinent she or he is not placing the proper value on the relationship

Don't Hurry

For one reason or another, more women aspire being married than men, which may bring an anxious spirit. Anxiousness leads to eagerness to do or have something because of fear or nervousness.

A tensed desire to be in a relationship or marriage can ignite an anxious spirit. Many times, it results in settling for less than what the woman is ordained for and what she deserves.

There are various reasons, for being anxious such as, being alone, getting older, financial support, and help with children.

Where Are You?

I prepared a power point relationship presentation; in that presentation is a circle entitled, Where Are You? The presentation explains seven stages of beginning a relationship. The first circle begins with contentment, the second, working on self; the third, waiting; the fourth, friendship; the fifth, dating; the sixth, relationship; the last is marriage. It is important knowing one's position in the circle and developing personal growth. As an illustration, it pertains to a person's desires in preparation for a relationship.

Although the circle begins with being content, some may experience another phase of the circle first. Being in a content stage can be a side effect of a dreadful marriage, failed relationship, or life experiences.

In other words, being content is a comfort zone and untimely disturbances may become chaotic. Additionally, when one is content it stimulates peace of mind, patience, and structure in one's life. The importance of being happy and aware of one's personal status is self-examination.

Therefore, the second phase of the circle is working on self. This is a never-ending process. Surely, there is always imperfections in our human lifestyles, personalities or characters. A necessary aspect of this phase is being willing to self-examine. When one is unwilling to admit weaknesses, it can lead to self-denial. Self-denial is damaging. Furthermore, realizing our faults and striving to improve each day keeps the relationship alive.

The third phase of the circle is waiting. Although each stage has its own significance the waiting stage is highly critical. We, as couples, seem to want what we desire instantly without hesitation. Waiting seems cumbersome, but it is rewarding.

Timing is essential, but God's timing perfects one's desires. Waiting is part of the process that exemplifies patience, and fortitude. Waiting means that a person does not settle for someone who she or he is not equally yoked with.

A man who has prayed and asked God to reveal his mate must wait until she is confirmed. He will know through circumstances and situations that she is sent from above.

God places the man to receive his mate. In fact, the man is taught about being the priest of his home, and how to love God. No doubt, when a man learns to love God he will know how to love his mate.

Next, a woman who is waiting is positioned by God to receive her mate. God teaches her patience and virtue.

The fourth phase of the circle is friendship. This phase should not be taken lightly. It is one of the most serious phases. The greatest problem that most couples experience in this phase is prematurely transitioning from friendship to the relationship phase. This causes a   dysfunctional relationship. Some couples exit the friendship stage and enter the dating stage. Whereas, finding out they should still be in the friendship phase.

When developing a relationship, the couple should be best friends. Consequently, as the friendship develops, an open and honest communication is easily expressed.

The fifth phase is Dating. Most couples begin in the relationship phase before the dating phase, which is out of order.

The dating phase is a semi-formal mode. In this phase couples go out and get to know each other's habits in formal and informal settings. On the whole, they observe each other's character. This phase is absent of intimacy. What is more, couples with children should not introduce their children to the person they are dating until that phase is finished.

The reason is, this phase of the relationship may not work. Furthermore, the next one may not work either. Thus, it is not good for children to meet multiple partners as a result of short term dating.

The sixth phase is the relationship. The relationship phase denotes that a commitment has been consummated. As a case in point, each party has agreed on being in an exclusive relationship. Now, is the proper time to introduce your mate to family, children, and friends. In this phase decisions are made about your future.

The seventh and final phase is the marriage phase. This phase is ultimately the pinnacle of each party, goals, and dreams. In this phase, each party recognizes that God has joined them. They have evaluated each other's pros and cons. They have communicated and agreed to strive and improve their weaknesses. Each couple agrees to

premarital counseling and periodic post marital
counseling.

Recognizing God's Gift

Sometimes a woman will not recognize God's gift because she has her own prerequisites or standards. It is understandable that a woman wants what she wants, but it is more important receiving whom God has ordained for her. Actually, many women adamantly desire their mates based on certain requirements. However, somehow these women forget that God will rectify what He has ordained.

On that note, I am not saying that God will not give a person the desires of the heart or give one less than what is requested, but sometimes it is not the person's expectations.

Not Believing But Still Receiving

There are some who might ask, "What about those who do not believe in God or do not serve Him?" My response is, "You are playing Russian roulette." When one's foundation is built solely upon personal requirements, and expectations many times it leads to a dysfunctional relationship.

How Do I meet Mr. Right?

Mr. Right is often by-passed because he is judged by his status. Many qualified men have been overlooked because of status quo opinions.

Mr. Right may not look like Denzel or have Boaz' finances, but may be an ordinary looking guy with an everyday job. The desire of many women is meeting Mr. Right or being enthrone by the man of their dreams. Contrary to that, Mr. Right seems to elude them.

Once the woman meets a man and the connection is strong, and he is seemingly the one she has prayed for, she then asks herself, "What is next?"

I advise women to pray and seek confirmation of the man who, in many situations, have suddenly appeared in their lives. It is necessary knowing if he is in her life for a reason, season, or lifetime.

As previously mentioned, there are many women who desire "being enthroned by the man of their dreams." Of course, expectations vary from woman to woman based on specific needs, beliefs, or background.

A friend mentioned that she asked women at a women's conference to list their prerequisites for a mate. All their lists were filled with expectations, while mine was blank. The reason is, when she told God what she "wanted this did not fit or work out." Furthermore, she decided to allow God to show her what His desire for her was. In particular, my friend stated, "The things I wanted for myself is not what God wanted for me."

That is powerful and it allows people to totally surrender to God's will and purpose for their lives. Many times, we as people, make plans, but God has to establish our steps.

Do Not Be Desperate and Lonely

The ratio of black men to women is usually in favor of the man. According to Adam Carlson in the AJC,

"Atlanta has about 80,000 more single women (ages 18-64) than single men – one of the largest such gaps in the country, according to an analysis of U.S. Census data." For this reason, many women become desperate and lonely. When some women become desperate they will settle for less than what has been ordained for them.

In many situations, she allows abuse and other forms of mistreatment to prevail in fear of not being alone or self-sufficient.

Often times when people become desperate, instead of receiving whom God has ordained for them, they settle for who wants them. When being in a relationship is a personal choice and not God's choice it can be hazardous.

God Positions The Woman

It is important that every woman desiring a mate allows God to position her to receive her best friend, spirit mate, and husband.

The woman should pray for the man she desires, to take his rightful place as the Priest of their marriage. Praying in advance for the mate can be beneficial.

Remember, God positions the woman and places the man!!! She must be in a proper place while receiving God's gift and blessing to her. Certainly, she is seeking God. Being in a place of contentment and not divulging in unnecessary relationships is of the upmost importance.

Mary was in a position to receive the greatest gift to mankind. She was not just the recipient of a husband, but she became the mother of the divine birth of Jesus. God chooses people who loves and serves Him.

The Man As Your Provider

There are some women who feel that being the provider means having your own or certain resources before marriage.

What is more, many women expect the man to be the sole provider of the home. While other women do not mind having a spouse whom they can share the expenses with.

Some situations dictate that the responsibilities are shared. Personally, I think that a man should provide for his wife, and if needed he should do what it takes. This may mean working two jobs. The couple should mutually agree as to what role each should partake. Every situation is different and wisdom must be displayed when these decisions are made.

In marriage, two became one flesh. In fact, it is stated in Scripture, "One can chase a thousand and two can chase ten thousand (Deuteronomy 32:30, paraphrase). It is much easier when the couple works together in oneness.

I asked a friend, Shameka, "Do you feel that the husband should be the sole provider in the home?" She responded, "The man does not have to have total responsibility, but if the woman cannot, the husband should be able too." I concur with her because every situation is different.

A man does not have to make more money than his wife to be the Priest of his home. Surely, he should be the responsible covering and a good manager of his domain. If his weaknesses are his wife's strengths, then she should be allowed to compliment him in those areas. Many women are looking for their Boaz. Most of the time the woman is actually saying, "I want a man who can provide for me financially."

Reiterating, the woman should not be looking, but receiving. Boaz noticed Ruth (Ruth 2:5), it could have been because she was a stranger, and he noticed her work ethics. The most glaring characteristic of Boaz is that he was chosen by God to be Ruth's husband. He was in the lineage of David and Christ. He was respected by his employees, he also prayed for and with them.

Why We Are Not Married?

There are countless relationships that have lingered seemingly for an unnecessary length of time. Longevity has its place, but should also have limitations. If the parties agree to prolong the courtship for personal reasons a delay is understandable.

First of all, I must admit that I am disappointed because so many couples do not allow God as the foundation of their relationship. It is saddening looking at relationships that just seem to tarry without any purpose other than companionship or financial support.

At some point, a couple knows whether or not they can coexist long term. When it is realized that the man has not proposed after a lengthy courtship, the relationship needs evaluating. This is especially true when one person is ready for holy matrimony.

Do not be deceived

The first stages of communication between interested parties consist of questions and answers. Initial conversations are times of openness and truthfulness, which shows the heart of both parties involved. The expectation of the male counterpart is transparency. He should allow the woman the opportunity to decide if she wants to accept what he has revealed about himself or not.

Unfortunately, in many situations there is deceit, half-truths, or no choice is given. Women must beware of the various facades men have.

Some Red Flags That Could Get Women's Attention

Just as men must be aware of Red Flags women should so should women.

1. He is abusive or had an abusive past.

2. He is lazy and will not work.

3. Inconsistency, say one thing and do another

4. Can't visit his house but he will come to your house

5. Won't answer phone at certain times.

6. Can only see you during the day.

A Decision Must Be Made

Sometimes it seems the most difficult thing for a woman to do is make a decision on the mate who is presented to her. There are certain questions that a woman must ask herself.

1. Is he the answer to my prayer?

2. Are we compatible spiritually, emotionally, physically and financially?

3. Does he respect me?

4. Does he have short term and long term goals?

5. Does he have a loving heart?

Recognizing Reasons For Dating

Some men date to date, some date to mate, while others date to marry. When a man dates to date most likely he is simply just frivolously intermingling with multiple women.

Furthermore, he is not serious about maintaining a harmonious relationship. From his point of view, living in the moment with no strings attached is not abnormal. There are times when he is open and not deceptive about his intentions. While others do not verbalize their objectives but their motives are obvious.

Some warning signs are, lack of communication, acting nonchalant, not returning a text, or calling when it is convenient for him.

There are also men who date to mate. I would venture to say that most men fall in this category. As previously discussed the ratio of men to women is in favor of the men.

When a man dates to mate, most likely he is not seeking a wife, but a companion. Most of the time it is a sexual escapade. Unfortunately, women become a piece of meat, a sex object, or a conquest. This man may also show a degree of compassion for the woman's feelings, pain, or past. Just the same, she still becomes an object or just another number on his list of seductions.

What is more, dating to mate can be precarious; especially, with all the diseases prevalent in today's society. It must be noted that the men in this category are more likely to "shack" or live with a woman and not marry her.

Unlike the man who dates to mate, the man who dates to date is less likely to be nonchalant, and will communicate with his mate. He will not try to intentionally cause hurt and pain to his mate.

Some men date to marry. This man is looking for his wife, his good thing. She is not a conquest, but is the answer to a request made to God.

He is seeking his help meet. The Hebrew word for Help Meet is Kenegdo. Ezer means aid or help. Ezer is found twenty-one times in the Hebrew bible, eight times it means savior and other places it means strength or help. kenegdo means, "fit for," it also means, "is corresponding to, "counterpart, equal to, or matching. Meet means to fit or correspond to. In essence, the revelation I have received is, the woman or the wife is her husband's helper, strength, and counterpart. For this reason, they resemble, compliment, and support each other. They recognize they have been blessed with different abilities and stewardship, but must work together as Equal Partners, helping each other become successful.

On the whole, Precious and I were entwined by God and with each other. He joined us together perfectly. She saw my vision and I saw hers. She was not concerned about my financial status because we were connected spiritually and we knew God was going to enlarge our territory.

It is crucial that the woman a man is seeking is fit as his counterpart, or is equal to him. For some people, "fit" means that the man is financially secure and able to support the woman. The type of woman he attracts may be waiting for a man of his statue.

In other words, he has things in perfect order. While "fit" for some women is, a man who does not have a great job with a diminutive income. Whereas, some women just want a hard-working man whom they recognize as God's gift.

Most important, he will love her unconditionally. Personally, the type of wife that I am seeking will know me spiritually and not by my lack of income. No doubt, she will see my vision and our vision will interlink to fulfill the purpose of our lives.

Adam and Eve served as our inaugural couple and God gave Adam is counterpart and his equal, which was perfectly fit for him from his rib. They were blessed by God and He made provision for them. When God connects couples or mates He will supply their needs as they walk in obedience, vision, and purpose.

Conclusion:

It is my goal to help develop lasting relationships and marriages. To provide answers, insight, and information for those seeking solutions. Precious Relationships also strive to help those heal who are hurting as a result of dysfunctional relationships or marriages .

Finding, Receiving, Falling In Love strives to address common issues that confront many men and women. Apparently, there is a lack of proper dating or relationship etiquette. For instance, men are increasingly being hunted and chased by seemingly impatient, desperate, and lonely women. What is more, many women are settling for less than they deserve because of the scarcity of eligible men.

Without a doubt, having a solid foundation is the life-line of any relationship or marriage. Personally, I have learned the importance of allowing God to be the foundation of any relationship.

There's nothing more gratifying than praying and asking God to reveal the mate you desire. It is even more gratifying when He reveals it to both parties.

It is also important to have effective communication, commitment, consistency, and love. Open communication and effective dialogue is important. Staying committed is essential; being loyal and dedicated to each other is vital.

Each party must continue doing the things that were exciting and unique in the early stages of the relationship. Yes, love is the back bone of every relationship. As a case in point, Love will allow forgiveness, healing, trust, and patience to prevail.

I pray that this book help you have a lasting relationship. Just remember every relationship is Precious!!!

About the Author

A. R. Neal, known as Neal by most, is a native of Atlanta, Ga. He attended D. T. Howard High School and Morehouse College. Neal began writing poetry while in elementary school, a talent he inherited from his mother, Ms. Ruby Neal. She wrote poetry until passing at the age of 92. Neal was inspired to write his first book in 2006, which is entitled, Am I A Man? It is based on life lessons learned on what it takes to become a mature husband and man. The lesson learned occurred after experiencing a life altering divorce.